THE HISTORY

OF

CATS

IN

101 OBJECTS

Media Lab Books
For inquiries, call 646-838-6637

Published by Topix Media Lab
14 Wall Street, Suite 4B, New York, NY 10005

Printed in China

ISBN-10: 1-942556-64-0
ISBN-13: 978-1-942556-64-0

CEO **Tony Romando**

VICE PRESIDENT OF BRAND MARKETING **Joy Bomba**
DIRECTOR OF FINANCE **Vandana Patel**
DIRECTOR OF SALES AND NEW MARKETS **Tom Mifsud**
MANUFACTURING DIRECTOR **Nancy Puskuldjian**
FINANCIAL ANALYST **Matthew Quinn**
BRAND MARKETING ASSISTANT **Taylor Hamilton**

EDITOR-IN-CHIEF **Jeff Ashworth**
CREATIVE DIRECTOR **Steven Charny**
PHOTO DIRECTOR **Dave Weiss**
MANAGING EDITOR **Courtney Kerrigan**
SENIOR EDITORS **Tim Baker, James Ellis**

CONTENT EDITOR **Kaytie Norman**
CONTENT DESIGNER **Eric Marquard**
CONTENT PHOTO EDITOR **Catherine Armanasco**
ART DIRECTOR **Susan Dazzo**
ASSOCIATE ART DIRECTOR **Rebecca Stone**
ASSISTANT MANAGING EDITOR **Holland Baker**
SENIOR DESIGNER **Michelle Lock**
DESIGNER **Danielle Santucci**
ASSISTANT PHOTO EDITOR **Jessica Ariel Wendroff**
ASSISTANT EDITORS **Trevor Courneen, Alicia Kort**
EDITORIAL ASSISTANT **Isabella Torchia**

CO-FOUNDERS **Bob Lee, Tony Romando**

"I have studied many philosophers and many cats. The wisdom of cats is infinitely superior."

—HIPPOLYTE TAINE, 19TH CENTURY FRENCH CRITIC AND HISTORIAN

Table *of* Contents

The *Fixation* *With* Felines

ATS ARE EVERYWHERE. An estimated 600 million cats exist in the world, and they've found homes everywhere but Antarctica. Up to 96 million cats are owned in the United States alone. This is especially impressive once their independent nature, mercurial tendencies and allergy-inducing dander are all taken into account. Perhaps this is because with their giant eyes, small noses and round faces, cats remind us of human babies—though it should be noted that the majority of cat owners would take offense at this superficial explanation, insisting that the love shared between a cat and its person is borne out of a much deeper bond. Whatever the reason, humans are endlessly fascinated by cats, and these 101 objects will explain at least a few of the reasons why. Each object in this chronicle of cats highlights a different facet of their past, explains an especially bewildering behavior (such as why cats cannot resist cardboard boxes), or examines how cats have become an unusually large part of the zeitgeist. Taken together, these 101 objects reveal the surprising history of cats and how their past has gotten so delightfully tangled up with our own.

Here, Kitty Kitty

While scientists disagree over whether they are truly domesticated, house cats have been living alongside humans for thousands of years.

Smilodon Fossil

AN ANCIENT cousin to modern day lions, cheetahs and house cats, the Smilodon was a genus of saber-toothed cat that walked the Earth during the Late Pleistocene era and disappeared about 10,000 years ago during the Quaternary extinction. Since 1932, hundreds of thousands of Smilodon fossils have been found in the La Brea Tar Pits of Los Angeles, allowing paleontologists to understand a great deal about these prehistoric predators. We now know that these saber-toothed cats had bobtails instead of long ones, meaning that rather than running down their meal like a cheetah, they likely attacked by lying in wait and charging once their prey emerged—much like a modern cat waiting out a mouse.

Tiger Jaw

IN MANY ways, the common house cat is essentially a scaled-down tiger. Both have strong forelimbs, flexible spines and tails for balance. Though there are a few proportional differences, domestic cats and tigers also share the same number of bones, vertebrae and teeth. The similarities in their jaws also point to the similarities in their unusual diets: Be it moose or mouse, cats exclusively eat meat. Most animals, even those we usually refer to as carnivores, are able to obtain protein from nuts and plants—a useful trait for when prey is hard to come by. But cats are hypercarnivores that can't digest the nutrients they need from plants and must obtain them from other animals' bodies—this is probably why they became such good predators (and pouncers).

Millet

AS YOU might have expected, humans did not truly domesticate cats, at least not in the same way they tamed goats and sheep. Instead, cats chose to become domesticated, living with or near humans to hunt the other small animals attracted to our crops and food stores. Evidence of this domestication goes back 5,300 years, to cat bones found among the ruins of a human settlement in central China. The people of this ancient settlement grew large amounts of millet, a small-seeded grass. Through testing the remains of cats and other animals, scientists were able to show that while rodents, dogs and pigs in the same area mostly ate millet, the cats' diets were primarily made up of animals that ate millet—likely the rodents. This is the first known example of cats acting as mousers for humans, and perhaps the impetus of their domestication.

Phoenician Cargo Ship

CATS ARE notorious for hating water, but they became ubiquitous around the world thanks to their prowess on boats. It's believed that Phoenician cargo ships brought the first cats to Europe around 900 B.C., along a trade route that included stops in France and England. Phoenicians had gained their independence from Egypt during a revolt about 200 years prior and took a big risk in smuggling cats out with them: The Ancient Egyptian punishment for exporting cats, which they revered, was death. However, their usefulness in catching pests aboard the ships as well as their value as tradeable goods (and furry friends) must have been worth the risk.

Systema Naturae, 10th Edition

IN 1758, Carl Linnaeus's updated tome of animal taxonomy did two very important things: It introduced binomial nomenclature as a means of naming organisms, and it gave the domestic cat its Latin name, *Felis catus.* While Linnaeus's original classifications of species have been reorganized in accordance with discoveries regarding biology and evolution, he is still considered the father of taxonomy—the 10th edition of *Systema Naturae* is widely regarded as the "starting point" of valid names for organisms.

ARCHIATR
ACAD.
L

SY
N

REG

CI
G

CHARAC
S

ROLI LINNÆI

UITIS DE STELLA POLARI,

GII, MED. & BOTAN. PROFESS. UPSAL.;
L. HOLMENS. PETROPOL. BEROL. IMPER.
MONSPEL. TOLOS. FLORENT. SOC.

STEMA
ATURÆ

PER

A TRIA NATURÆ,

SECUNDUM

SSES, ORDINES,
ERA, SPECIES,

CUM

RIBUS, DIFFERENTIIS.
ONYMIS, LOCIS.

TOMUS I

The "MUNCHKINS" Hollywood Star

MUNCHKIN CATS, rumored to be named after the equally short-legged natives of Munchkinland in *The Wizard of Oz*, are a relatively new breed of American cat that can trace their roots to the early 1980s. A stray with the genetic mutation for unusually short legs gave birth to kittens in a sympathetic Louisiana woman's backyard, and by 1990 there were litters of examples. Though controversial—some believe purposefully breeding these cats encourages physical deformities—the breed was formally recognized by The International Cat Association in 1994.

Scale

DEVISED OUT of necessity for trading goods, scales have existed since around 5000–6000 B.C. Both Ancient Egyptian and Babylonian civilizations used equal arm balances, and scales relied on some sort of counterweight until the late 18th century, when the spring scale was invented. Though spring scales are still manufactured, the most accurate scales available today use electronics—allowing us to understand just how overweight some domestic cats have become. Due to lack of portion control and being given little opportunity or incentive to exercise, many indoor cats are tipping the scales toward morbid obesity. In fact, animal obesity experts at the University of Tennessee College of Veterinary Medicine have restructured their Body Fat Index charts to reflect the new reality: While the old chart had a maximum of 45 percent body fat, the new chart goes beyond 70 percent.

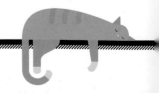

Cat Crazy

*Mankind has been holding cats
in high esteem for at least 4,000 years, a tradition
of respect that continues to this day.*

Bastet Statue

THE ADORATION of cats can be traced as far back as ancient Egypt, where felines were both celebrated and protected by law. Originally a leonine warrior goddess, Bastet eventually became the protector goddess of cats and was subsequently depicted as a cat-headed woman.

Great Sphinx of Giza

THE GREAT SPHINX, with a man's head and a lion's body, was carved into the bedrock of a plateau. Commonly believed to have been built in the third millennium B.C., the 240-foot-long, 66-foot-tall feline hybrid is as puzzling as cats themselves: When exactly did it happen? Why was it built, and by whom? What happened to its nose, and did a cat have something to do with its destruction? These questions, known collectively as the Riddle of the Sphinx, may never have satisfactory answers.

Bathroom Sink

DUE TO the expense of installing indoor plumbing and general ignorance regarding the effects of poor hygiene, sinks with running water were virtually nonexistent in the home until a relatively recent point in human history. It wasn't until Louis Pasteur's studies during the 1860s on the effects of bacteria that people realized the health benefits of indoor plumbing greatly outweighed the financial cost. As a result, the bathroom sink equipped with a drain and faucet wasn't commonplace until the early 1900s—at which point cats everywhere likely began to annoy their owners by jumping in just when they'd started to wash up for the day.

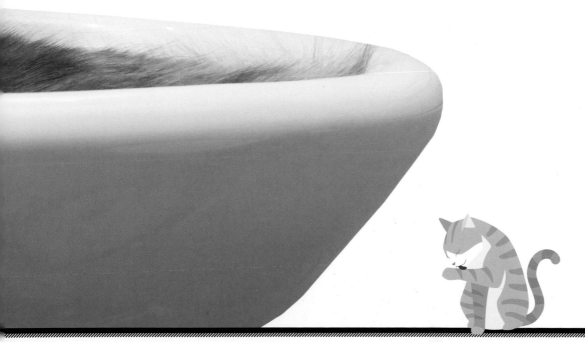

Mummified Cat

WHILE SOME cats may have been mummified to be buried with their owners, most were embalmed and wrapped as an offering to the gods. Archaeologists believe between about 332 B.C. and 30 B.C., Ancient Egyptian priests made a profit from raising cats and turning them into offerings, which people could

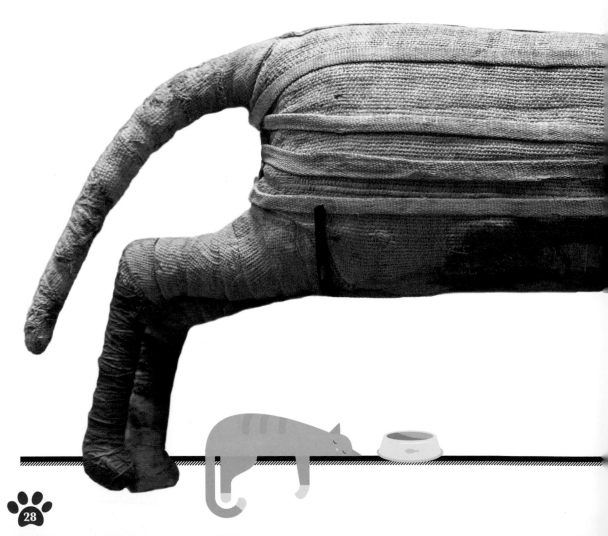

then buy for their own use. For clients on a budget, priests made cat mummies that contained just a few bones. But if someone was aiming to make a more impressive sacrifice to Bastet—Egyptian goddess of fire, cats, the home and pregnant women—they could purchase an entire mummified cat.

Ancient Roman Cat Mosaic

STARTING AROUND the 5th century A.D., Romans held cats in exceptionally high regard, associating them with liberty and divinity, and even allowing them to roam freely through temples. Ancient Romans had respected cats for their hunting prowess since an even earlier time—this mosaic is from the second century B.C. As a result, feline mosaics from this period can be found throughout cities as far apart as Pompeii and Istanbul.

FREYA IN HER CHARIOT.

Illustration Of Freya

"When she goes on a journey she sits in a chariot drawn by two cats."
—Snorri Sturluson, Prose Edda

GODDESS OF love, fertility and marriage, Freya was a highly revered Norse deity. When she wasn't riding a boar with golden bristles, she traveled in a chariot drawn by cats given to her by Thor. According to Norse mythology, she was so fond of her cats that, much like any cat owner, she blessed anyone who was kind to them.

Maneki-neko

KNOWN IN English as a welcoming cat, fortune cat or money cat, maneki-neko is a common sight in Japanese and Chinese businesses everywhere. While collectors argue whether the conspicuous Japanese cat first appeared in Tokyo or Kyoto during the 17th or 18th century or whether there's any significance in which paw is raised, the origin story remains more or less the same: One day, a poor shop owner took in a starving cat. After the owner fed and cared for it, the cat began sitting outside the shop and gesturing to anyone who walked by. The owner's fortune turned around, and ever since, the beckoning cat has been considered a lucky talisman for small business owners.

Tashirojima Cat Shrine

ON A small island off the east coast of Japan, cats are treated the way they deserve to be—like royalty. Tashirojima, or Cat Island, as it has been nicknamed, is home to about 100 people but many hundreds of cats. It's also the site of a cat shrine, likely erected and renovated between the 18th and 19th century by fishermen who considered the cats on the island to be a source of good luck. Fascinated cat-lovers can visit the shrine and stay overnight in a cat-shaped cabin, but leave your pooch at home: Tashirojima is a dog-free island.

Crystal Palace

THE CRYSTAL Palace was originally built in Hyde Park, London, to house the Great Exhibition of 1851. In 1854 the Crystal Palace was relocated to South London, where it was the site of many grand events until destroyed by a fire in 1936. In addition to becoming the world's first theme park and hosting various festivals and concerts, the Crystal Palace was also the site of the world's first large-scale organized cat show in 1871. Approximately 160 cats were in attendance and were judged by groups according to color. The show was a huge success, igniting a trend of larger and larger cat shows in Britain and, eventually, the first official cat show at Madison Square Garden in 1895.

Towser Monument

TOWSER, a female tortoiseshell cat who was owned by Scotland's Glenturret Distillery, has the distinct honor of holding the Guinness World Record for Greatest Mouser. Averaging three mice per day in her lifespan of more than 20 years, it's estimated that Towser caught 28,899 mice. After she passed away in 1987, the distillery Towser worked so hard to keep mouse-free honored her with a bronze statue and by using her paw prints in the bottle design of one of their whiskies, Fairlie's Light Highland Liqueur.

TOWSER
21 APRIL 1963 – 20 MARCH 1987
TOWSER THE FAMOUS CAT WHO LIVED IN THE STILL
HOUSE GLENTURRET DISTILLERY FOR ALMOST 24
YEARS. SHE CAUGHT 28,899 MICE IN HER LIFETIME
WORLD MOUSING CHAMPION GUINNESS BOOK OF RECORDS

Kit-Cat Clock

PRACTICALLY AS common as cats themselves, the Kit-Cat Clock is a timeless piece of Americana. The classic art deco clock with a pendulum tail was invented in 1932, but it wasn't until a few tweaks in its design a couple of decades later that the Kit-Cat Clock became cemented as one of the most iconic novelties from the '50s. Kit-Cat Clocks are now sold all over the world, and according to the manufacturer, one has been purchased every three minutes for the past 50 years.

Cat-Eye Glasses

A POPULAR style from the '50s and '60s (the same time period when the advent of kitty litter allowed people to keep their cats indoors permanently—coincidence?), upswept "cat-eye" glasses were famously worn by trendsetters such as Grace Kelly, Elizabeth Taylor and Marilyn Monroe, and likely anyone who has ever decided to wear their hair in a beehive. However, it was Audrey Hepburn's iconic pair of "Manhattans" in *Breakfast at Tiffany's* that catapulted this style of eyewear into the spotlight.

Windows

WHILE THE very first "windows" were essentially holes in a wall, Romans are credited with being the first to place glass in their windows around 100 A.D.—a great improvement over the prior practice of using animal hide or cloth. However, this glass likely wasn't very transparent, and the Roman methods of window making were lost during the Dark Ages. It wasn't until the 17th century that the French perfected a method to make large panels of clear glass, to the joy of curious cats around the world. In addition to having a clear view of birds, squirrels and everything else that moves, glass windows afforded cats the ability to nap in a sunny spot, undisturbed by the rest of the world.

Cat Fancy Magazine

UBIQUITOUS IN veterinary office waiting rooms and on coffee tables of cat lovers all over the U.S., *Cat Fancy* enjoyed the title of longest-running cat magazine until its final (50th anniversary) issue in March 2015. The magazine was intended, obviously, for cat fanciers and contained a wealth of information regarding cat shows, breeders and general cat care and welfare. Now *Cat Fancy* has started its second life under a new name, *Catster*—a magazine that still offers tidbits on cat care, but largely focuses on the fun, whimsical side of our feline friends.

Kittens

CAT FANCY

THE AUTHORITY OF ALL THINGS CAT

NORWEGIAN FOREST CAT: Loving Companion

ut Down **NY Subway**

LaPerm:
Curly-Coated Cutie

TFANCY

APRIL 2014

Kittens!

Best AGE to Spay

What to FEED

22

Hello Kitty Coin Purse

CREATED BY Yuko Shimizu and produced by the Japanese company Sanrio, Hello Kitty first emerged with the introduction of a simple vinyl coin purse in 1975. The brand is now a worldwide merchandising phenomenon, with everything from paper towels to panini makers to planes in Taiwan emblazoned with the cute and quirky catlike girl.

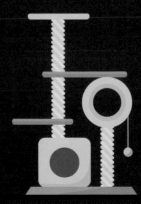

23

Cat Ears

FOR SOME WOMEN, donning black cat ears and a faux tail isn't just for Halloween—it's an everyday fashion statement. Cat ears spiked in popularity during the '40s and '50s, likely because of the creation of Catwoman and, on the other side of the globe, the growing popularity of Japanese manga that featured "nekomimi," or "catgirls." It's unclear why manga authors created so many feline-human hybrid characters, though it's not exactly surprising. Perhaps even more than most of the world, Japanese culture has long been captivated by cats. Today, the simplicity of a pair of cat ears make them a go-to accessory for costume parties and a foolproof Halloween accessory for the budget-conscious trick-or-treater.

Paws For Concern

Cats have been revered in certain times and cultures, but due to various myths and legends (and their very real propensity for killing small animals in large numbers), they've been reviled in others.

24

Cat Sìth Illustration

A GAELIC myth, the Cat Sìth (pronounced "caught shee") was a fairy creature said to resemble a black cat with a white spot on its chest. Legends of the Scottish Cat Sìth were more common than the Irish Cait Sidhe, but both were said to steal a person's soul in the time between death and burial, when the soul would be claimed by the gods. It was also rumored that the Cat Sìth could become a witch capable of transforming into a cat. The witch could do this eight times, but if it chose to become a cat for a ninth time, it would remain so forever. This might be the origin of another legend: "Cats have nine lives."

Pope Gregory IX's Papal Bulla

IN 1232, Pope Gregory IX issued the papal bull *Vox in Rama*, authenticated with his personal papal bulla—a lead seal. *Vox in Rama* was an edict which condemned the Luciferian heresy, a form of devil worship. The bull warned of the initiation rites of the Satanic cult: People were first approached by a toad, goose or duck. Then they would meet a slender, pale man who would make them forget all about their faith. Later a black cat would appear and walk backwards with its tail erect. While *Vox in Rama* did not call for the extermination of black cats, it's often credited as the origin of cat persecution in the Middle Ages.

Kattenstoet Float

ON MARCH 13, 1938, the town of Ypres, Belgium, held its first Kattenstoet. Also known as the Cat Parade, Kattenstoet is a symbolic recreation of the town's previous practice of annually tossing live cats from a tower—a tradition that went as far back as 1127 A.D., according to some accounts, and was carried on until 1817. Thankfully, reports indicate the very last cat thrown survived the fall. There is little definitive proof to explain why the barbaric practice intitially began, though it may have originally been a means of culling an overwhelming feral cat population. The Cat Parade has experienced a few hiatuses since its inception, but it has occurred annually since 1955 and is now held on the second Sunday of May each year. Though each celebration ends with a tongue-in-cheek tossing of toy cats from the Hall tower, most of the day celebrates felines: The parade includes tableaux depicting themes such as the history of cat worship, cats in language and legend and cats around the world, as well as cat-centric costumes and floats.

27

Witch Drawing
c. 1600

"You see, a witch has to have a familiar, some little animal like a cat or a toad. He helps her somehow. When the witch dies the familiar is supposed to die too, but sometimes it doesn't. Sometimes, if it's absorbed enough magic, it lives on."
—HENRY KUTTNER, *BEFORE I WAKE…*

FOR THE majority of the Middle Ages, people lived in fear of witches and their "familiars," the animals that were connected to them. As demonstrated in this illustration from the turn of the 17th century, cats—especially black cats—were commonly suspected of being in cahoots with witches. Belief in witchcraft began to decline greatly during the Age of Enlightenment—in 1735, Great Britain's Parliament passed the Witchcraft Act, which made it a crime to accuse others of possessing magical powers or practicing witchcraft. France had passed a similar law in 1682, as would Poland in 1776. On top of protecting people from being a defendant in a witch trial, these acts were also an important stepping stone for cats, helping them make the transition from "devil's accomplice" to "cuddly companion."

Cat Piano

AN 1883 issue of the French science magazine *La Nature* featured a cat piano, an imaginary organ played by pricking cats' tails with a nail, similar to a piano's hammer hitting a string. While designs of cat pianos have been seen since the late 16th century, there is—mercifully—no evidence that one has ever been built. Unsurprisingly, the earliest images of cat pianos show them being used in witches' rituals. But in 1803, German medical scientist Johann Christian Reil (who would later coin the term "psychiatry") posited that the cat piano could be used to treat patients who had lost their ability to focus—presumably, if the sound of 88 cats wailing in disharmony didn't grab their attention, nothing would.

Stephens Island Wren

NOW EXTINCT, the demise of the Stephens Island wren was initially credited to a cat named Tibbles. In 1894, a man named David Lyall moved to the small island off the southern coast of New Zealand, bringing his cat with him. Tibbles enjoyed hunting the small flightless birds native to the island, and regularly brought them to Lyall. Curious about the birds, Lyall sent a specimen to England, where bird expert Sir Walter Buller declared it a new species of wren. Unfortunately, as the legend goes, Tibbles's prowess led the Stephens Island wren to extinction within the year. While it's currently contested whether Tibbles is solely responsible for eradicating this species of wren, she certainly deserves a portion of the blame.

Toilet

MORE THAN 200 years after its invention in 1596, the flush toilet finally became widespread in the 1850s—convenience and cleanliness ultimately prevailed over the prohibitive cost and perceived embarrassment of having a private room dedicated to relieving oneself; previously, chamber pots were considered much more discreet. Unfortunately for most cat owners, the idea of ever having privacy is laughable, even in the bathroom—with moving water, an unusual flushing sound and, by virtue of the fact that you would rather they leave it alone, many cats are fascinated by the toilet. Especially when you're sitting on it.

31

Bird Feathers

"The reason cats climb is so that they can look down on almost every other animal—it's also the reason they hate birds." —K.C. BUFFINGTON

WHILE FERAL cats must hunt in order to feed themselves, house cats don't lose their predatory instinct just because kibble is always there. Like adorable little addicts, the need to hunt is compulsive—a full stomach is unlikely to stop a cat from pouncing on passing prey, even if they don't end up eating it. Estimates made in 2013 from the Smithsonian Conservation Biology Institute suggest that of the 84 million cats owned by Americans, up to 47 million of them are active hunters. Between feral and pet cats, between 1.4 and 3.7 billion birds are killed per year, with pet cats being responsible for about one-third of these bird deaths. Fortunately, an array of fake feathered trinkets are available for indoor cats who need to scratch that itch.

Purrfect Pets

Because they love their pets (and their couch, carpet and curtains), cat owners—especially those with indoor cats—have an arsenal of accessories and supplies to keep their charges healthy and happy.

32

Musket Balls

CATS MADE their way around the world aboard ships, earning their keep by making sure the vessels did not become overrun with rats. It's clear cats became valued shipmates, resulting in superstitions regarding their presence (or lack thereof) and various nautical phrases such as "cat-o-nine tails," "catwalk" and "cats paws." When the cats weren't catching rats or napping, it seems that crew members enjoyed playing with them: There are accounts of sailors fashioning toys out of the only scrap material around—musket balls and twine—for their furry first mates.

Ball of Yarn

YARN HAS an incredibly long history: The oldest known yarn artifacts are string skirts, dated from up to 20,000 years ago. Twisted by hand until about 5,000 B.C., yarn was revolutionized when rudimentary spindles were invented—spinning wheels, which allowed for far faster production, wouldn't arrive until approximately 500–1000 A.D. Scores of improvements were made over the centuries, and as production methods of yarn became more evolved and less labor intensive, yarn itself became less expensive—a great victory for curious kittens all over the world.

Catnip

THE CATNIP plant, otherwise known as *Nepeta cataria*, is an herb belonging to the mint family. Humans have been using catnip as far back as Ancient Rome, where it was an herbal medicine for ailments such as headaches, scabies and insomnia. Catnip was introduced to America in the 18th century—a recipe for medicinal tea dating from 1712 Massachusetts includes catnip as a key ingredient. Somewhere along the way, humans noticed cats were attracted to this medicinal plant—specifically, the chemical compound in the herb that affects cats is called nepetalactone. Though only about 50 percent of cats respond to catnip, those that do seemingly react with their entire being: When sniffed, it produces a high, and when eaten it acts as a mild kitty sedative.

Spratt's Cat Food

"Entirely supersedes the unwholesome practice of feeding boiled horse flesh; keeps cat in perfect health."
    –SPRATT'S PATENT CAT FOOD ADVERTISEMENT, 1876

UNTIL THE late 1800s, pet cats subsisted on table scraps and whatever they hunted for themselves. But in 1860, a man from Ohio named James Spratt invented the first commercial food for dogs, and soon after, he extended his product line to include feline grub as well. Even still, buying food exclusively for your pet continued to be considered a luxury until post World War II, when companies such as Lipton, Carnation and Nabisco began to market their own pet food.

Bell Collar

WHILE THE sight of a cat with a bell on its collar is quite common, their use is rather controversial in the cat community. Though their purpose is to prevent cats from killing wildlife, critics argue that the bell isn't all that effective in warning prey and may in fact pose a danger to the cat, either by increasing the likelihood it will get stuck somewhere or by alerting a larger predator of its presence. On the other paw, owners may find a bell useful for locating a kitten—or even a larger cat—that has hidden itself away or gotten itself trapped in an unexpected spot, as cats are wont to do.

37

Kitty Litter

PRIOR TO the invention of cat litter, pet cats roamed in and out of houses as they pleased, and owners used sand, sawdust or wood shavings when it was necessary to keep them inside—though none of these were particularly effective in masking the stench of cat urine. In 1947, a man named Edward Lowe realized that granulated clay, with the ability to absorb its weight in water, worked far better than these alternatives. He began marketing it as Kitty Litter, and as a result, keeping cats entirely indoors was a realistic option—and one many people began to choose, creating a market for kitty litter innovations (clumping cat litter was introduced in the 1980s), countless toys, scratchers and even specialized "indoor" cat food.

38

Feather Teaser

FOR THE indoor cat that will never experience the joy of pouncing on a real live bird (or for owners who aren't interested in watching their playful pet's predatory instincts jut violently to the fore), the experience can be replicated with feather teasers. The varieties of cat teasers are endless, with many featuring brightly colored feathers, shiny fabric, bells and even faux birds to catch, bat around and rip apart. These upgrades, however, are surely designed for the owner more than the cat, as most felines are likely to swat at anything and everything dangled in their line of sight.

39

Scratching Post

FOR THOSE WHO ENJOY the company of felines, a scratching post is a necessity to keep curtains, sofas, wallpaper, doors, sheets, toilet paper and just about anything else a cat can dig its claws into from becoming kitty confetti. It's unclear when exactly the scratching post became commonplace, though it's likely within the last 60 years—domesticated cats still spent the majority of their time outdoors prior to the 1950s.

Cabinets

IN THE 1920s, an engineer and mother of 12 named Lillian Moller Gilbreth (who also happened to invent the shelves inside refrigerator doors and the foot-pedal trash can) interviewed more than 4,000 women to determine the ideal height for stoves, sinks and other kitchen appliances. No cats were involved in the interview process—not that it stops them from jumping, climbing and otherwise forcing themselves onto the tallest of household wares. Gilbreth's work emphasized efficiency and informed much of modern kitchen design, including the rising popularity of built-in cabinets. By the 1960s built-in cabinets were standard, and growing numbers of indoor cats began climbing inside them.

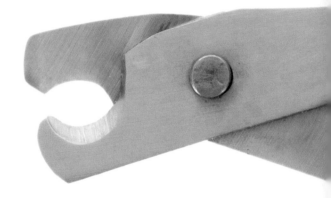

41

Nail
Clippers

NAIL CLIPPERS are a relatively recent invention: Clippers for humans were not patented until around 1876, and the earliest patent for animal nail clippers was filed in 1959. Feral cats never have their nails clipped, after all, and pet cats who lived out the majority of their days outdoors would spend enough time scratching and walking on rough surfaces to naturally file down their nails. However, once pampered pets began spending their days walking on rugs instead of rocks, owners began to realize that a scratching post was not enough to get the job done. In lieu of the expensive and controversial practice of declawing, most owners opt to periodically trim their cat's nails—an often risky endeavor.

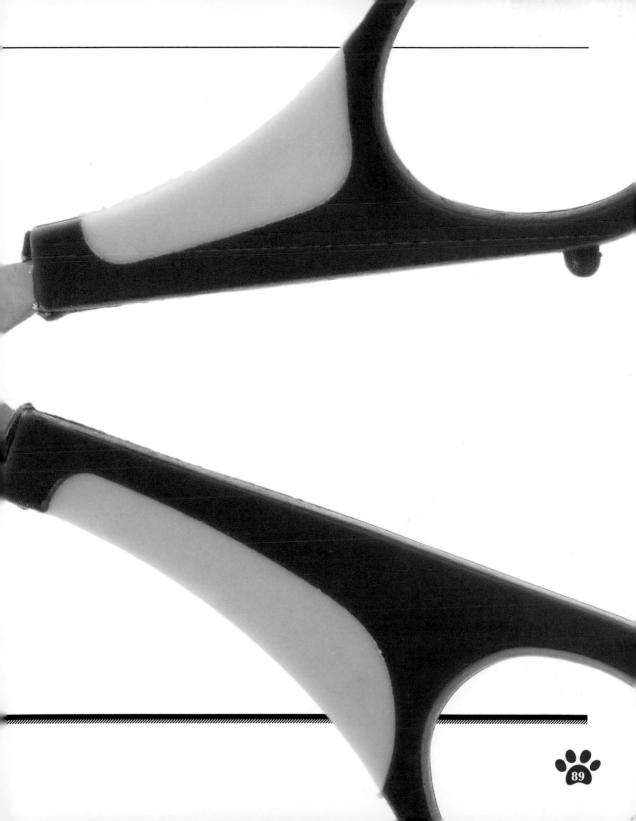

42

Toy Mouse

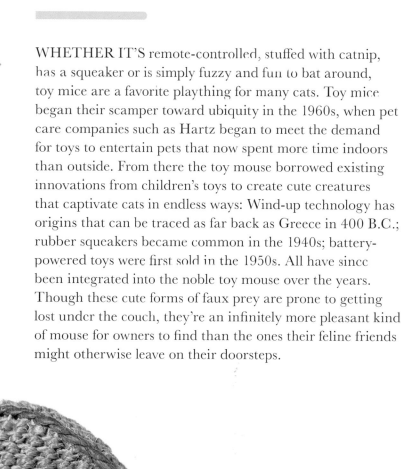

WHETHER IT'S remote-controlled, stuffed with catnip, has a squeaker or is simply fuzzy and fun to bat around, toy mice are a favorite plaything for many cats. Toy mice began their scamper toward ubiquity in the 1960s, when pet care companies such as Hartz began to meet the demand for toys to entertain pets that now spent more time indoors than outside. From there the toy mouse borrowed existing innovations from children's toys to create cute creatures that captivate cats in endless ways: Wind-up technology has origins that can be traced as far back as Greece in 400 B.C.; rubber squeakers became common in the 1940s; battery-powered toys were first sold in the 1950s. All have since been integrated into the noble toy mouse over the years. Though these cute forms of faux prey are prone to getting lost under the couch, they're an infinitely more pleasant kind of mouse for owners to find than the ones their feline friends might otherwise leave on their doorsteps.

43

Spray Bottle

"I had been told that the training procedure with cats was difficult. It's not. Mine had me trained in two days." —BILL DANA

UNLIKE VIRTUALLY every other pet, cats are neither easily trainable nor containable, leaving most owners to change their own behavior rather than the other way around. However, one device that deters most bad kitty behavior, if only momentarily, is the spray bottle. The trigger spray bottle was invented in the 1960s, mostly for cleaning purposes. But it also allows cat caretakers to discourage their charges from knocking over glasses, scratching the sofa or chewing on electrical cords—and even better, they can be used a safe distance away from any swiping claws.

44

Cat Condo

"The invention provides an answer to problems that are commonly faced by cat owners who esteem their pets to the point of housing them within their own dwellings in contrast to keeping them on the outside."
— FRANK L. CROW, PATENT US3479990 A, 1968

THE CAT condo, also known as a cat tree, kitty condo or cat stand, is an often unsightly piece of "cat furniture" meant to give cats their own space to nap, scratch, play, perch or hide. While such a piece would have been considered absurd until the mid-20th century, the increasing trend of keeping kitties indoors at all times necessitated an outlet for their intrinsic needs to scratch, climb and curl up in small spaces. According to a patent filed by Frank L. Crow in 1968, the cat tree would meet all of these needs and also function as an "attractive room accessory" that could be "color-coordinated with room-decorations." The cat condo has come a long way since the first iteration, with versions towering more than six feet tall and featuring lifelike leaves, hammocks and chic, streamlined designs.

Fancy Feast

FOUNDED IN 1982, Fancy Feast pioneered the concept of "decadent" wet cat food. Traditionally sold in small gold cans and shown in commercials being passionately eaten by a perfectly coiffed silver Persian, Fancy Feast has achieved the goal of making entrées such as "Grilled Liver & Chicken Feast in Gravy" look downright indulgent. In addition to their classic patés, flaked and grilled selections, refined cats can now also enjoy an array of broths and entrées infused with aged cheddar.

Cat Dancer

A DECEPTIVELY simple toy that's still popular today, the Cat Dancer was named the first nationally marketed interactive cat toy in 1983. Made from steel wire and rolled cardboard, the lure is intended to be held by humans on one end and batted by cats on the other. The springy nature of the wire makes it bob around once hit by a paw, meaning lazy owners need not do more than sit on the couch and hold out the toy in order to entertain a bored kitty. In a market full of remote-controlled toys, movies of wildlife footage and even interactive tablet games, the Cat Dancer is a reminder that cats will play with just about anything.

You Gotta be Kitten Me

While some may argue society spends too much time and money on felines, cat lovers would likely disagree.

Laser Pointer

THOUGH THE question of who invented the laser is contentious, there's no doubt the original concept came from Albert Einstein and his studies on light waves. In 1977 the first laser was patented by Gordon Gould, and by the 1990s, laser pointers were extremely affordable and found everywhere from board rooms and classrooms to keychains. In 1993, Kevin T. Amiss and Martin H. Abbott filed a patent for using a laser pointer as a "method for exercising a cat." According to Amiss and Abbott, "Cats are not characteristically disposed toward voluntary aerobic exercise. It becomes the burden of the cat owner to create situations of sufficient interest to the feline to induce even short-lived and modest exertion for the health and well-being of the pet." Thanks to Einstein, we have one more hilarious, hi-tech method of exercising a cat that doesn't feel burdensome at all.

Sauvignon Blanc

MAKING WINE from sauvignon blanc grapes dates back to 18th-century France, where the variety became popular in the Loire Valley and Bordeaux wine region. The aroma of a sauvignon blanc often includes notes of grass, minerals, fruit and—due to the breakdown of these grapes releasing the same pheromones as cats—cat urine. Though this sounds as though it would be off-putting, many humans are oddly attracted to the scent—something perfume makers have known for centuries. Studies have shown that people who find this smell pleasant are more likely to be infected with a parasite called *Toxoplasma gondii*; a parasite transmitted by cats. While it's mostly harmless to adult humans (this parasite is the reason why pregnant women are excused from litter box duty), rats infected with toxoplasmosis also become attracted to cat urine—an obvious advantage for the purring predator.

Cat Hammock

ALTHOUGH CAT-WORSHIP has declined marginally since Ancient Egyptian times, cat caretakers have never stopped pampering their furry friends and investing in a variety of household furniture additions to make their cats' lives as comfortable and enjoyable as possible. An example of this habit is perfectly manifest in the cat hammock—a miniature version of the tree-swinging summertime lounger for humans. Cat hammocks were often strung up by sailors to give the ship's mouser a

place to snooze and have since become more popular landside as DIY projects, with people constructing the beds out of whatever materials they have lying around. One such person is Martha Stewart, who on an episode of *Martha Stewart Living* in 2000 made a cat hammock using a carpet sample and some chain. While many people still build their own or buy homemade hammocks from Etsy, companies such as Cat Crib have been selling them since 2012.

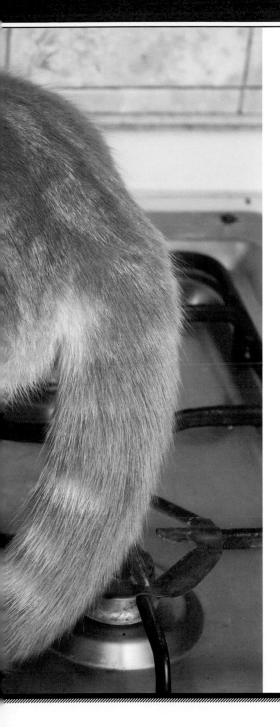

Stove

"If a cat sits on a hot stove, that cat won't sit on a hot stove again. That cat won't sit on a cold stove either. That cat just don't like stoves." —MARK TWAIN

STOVES HAVE always been ideal appliances for fulfilling three basic cat needs: They are warm, they present the opportunity to swipe a morsel (or more) of something tasty and they offer a great vantage point to survey the kitchen. Though it made little difference to cats, who surely enjoyed curling up near wood-fired stoves just fine, humans greatly benefited from the invention of the gas stove during the 1820s British Industrial Revolution. By the 1930s, the electric stove had become a common option as well.

Wall-Mounted Perch

AT THEIR MOST BASIC, wall-mounted cat perches are essentially bookshelves, which were invented out of storage necessity after the printing press made books more accessible in the 15th century. Because cats try to climb everything in sight, there's no doubt they've been climbing on bookshelves ever since Gutenberg's invention led to their necessity. Climbing is a way for kittens to work on their balance while developing their flexibility, and it also gives cats a clear vantage point from which to survey their surroundings. For households with more than one animal, climbing even gives cats the opportunity to increase their territory. To meet a cat's intrinsic need to climb, many owners have taken to installing these special shelves lined with non-slip materials meant just for that purpose. The wall-mounted perch's space-saving features and relatively chic look have made it a popular fixture in small spaces with feline roommates.

The Birthday Cake, Harry Whittier Frees

"There's no need for a piece of sculpture in a home that has a cat."   —WESLEY BATES

THE PRACTICE of dressing up one's cat and taking adorable pictures is, to the chagrin of many felines, more than 100 years old. Popularized by Harry Whittier Frees, early costumes for pets seem to have mostly been miniature versions of everyday human clothes. While dressing up animals as regular people is still hilarious today (as evidenced by countless blogs, articles and memes focused on such pictures), modern cat owners may choose to turn their pets into miniature celebrities, other animals, superheroes or food—we're only limited by our imaginations (and each cat's individual tolerance level).

Automatic Feeder

"Never ask a hungry cat whether he loves you for yourself alone."
–Louis Camuti

AUTOMATED PET feeders hit the market surprisingly soon after commercial dog and cat food took off. Unlike modern pet feeders, which store enough food for multiple feedings and dispense a small amount at a time, the first pet feeders from the 1940s only served one meal. Intended for busy pet owners who might have been away whenever their beloved kitty expected dinner, it worked via an alarm clock. When the alarm went off, a tray of food either slid into view from underneath its cover or was revealed by a lid that popped up, and voilà! Dinner was served (unless, of course, it had already been eaten by a persistent kitty).

54

Centre d'Enseignement et de Recherches
de
Médecine Aéronautique

Merci pour votre participation à mon succès du 18 Octobre 1963

Félicette

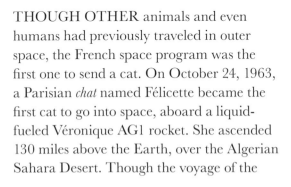

Véronique
Rocket

THOUGH OTHER animals and even humans had previously traveled in outer space, the French space program was the first one to send a cat. On October 24, 1963, a Parisian *chat* named Félicette became the first cat to go into space, aboard a liquid-fueled Véronique AG1 rocket. She ascended 130 miles above the Earth, over the Algerian Sahara Desert. Though the voyage of the "Astrocat" was quick—she returned just 15 minutes after entering space—it was extremely useful for French scientists, who studied Félicette's brain waves to determine whether space travel had affected her. Though Félicette has not made the same mark on history as the animals who traveled to space before her, she certainly made one large step for catkind.

Frank Lloyd Wright Cat House

FAMED FOR iconic architectural designs such as Fallingwater and New York's Guggenheim Museum, Frank Lloyd Wright was also commissioned for smaller projects—as small as 4 square feet, in fact. In the early 1950s, the Gerald B. Tonkens family of Cincinnati commissioned Wright for the construction of a house for their cat. The design was rendered by Thomas Olsen, the site supervisor, under the direction of Wright, who described his vision for the cat house to Olsen over a phone call. The Cat House features an ultra-modern design typical of the mid-20th century and is painted Cherokee Red, one of Wright's signature colors. In 2014, the Cat House was acquired by the Cat Fanciers' Association Foundation, Inc., and is now on display at the Feline Historical Museum in Alliance, Ohio.

Fire Engine

PERHAPS THE cutest part of a firefighter's day is climbing up their ladder to rescue a kitten that's gotten stuck in a tree. However, fire engines did not always come with ladders—in fact, the earliest "fire engines" from the 1700s weren't engines at all, but water pumps on wheels. In the 19th century, most firefighters carried their equipment via horse and carriage, and in 1911, Mack Trucks began producing

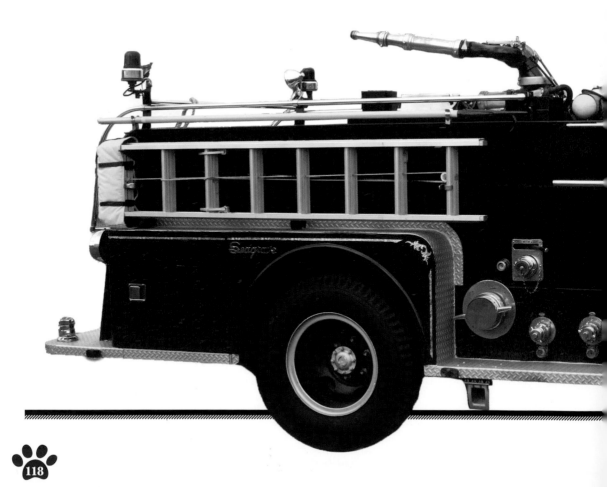

fire trucks with engines. Ladders were not added until the 1930s, when the construction of taller buildings demanded greater reach. All of the elements of a modern fire truck were designed in the 1960s, including enclosed seating, modern water pumps, extendable ladders and "cherry pickers," which are particularly helpful when your beloved tabby has found a favored perch in a 40-foot tree.

Vegan Cat Food

"Trying to feed a cat a vegan diet would be like me feeding my horses meat. You're taking a whole species of animal and trying to force it to eat something that it isn't designed to handle."
—LEW OLSON, PH.D., AUTHOR OF *RAW AND NATURAL NUTRITION FOR DOGS*

CATS ARE categorized as hypercarnivores and lack the ability to obtain all the nutrients they need from most non-meat proteins, which makes vegan cat food sound like an oxymoron. Undeterred by such biological obstacles, diehard animal lovers have found a controversial way to feed their flesh-loving kitties a meat-free diet: plant-based supplements. One such supplement, Vegecat, has been on the market since 1986. While most veterinarians advise against feeding cats a vegan diet and caution that relying on supplements leaves a lot of room for error, there is anecdotal evidence of cats thriving on such a diet.

58

Meow Parlour

THE VERY first cat café, called Cat Flower Garden, opened in Taiwan in 1998. But it wasn't until a cat café opened in Japan in 2005 that they really took off—because many rental apartments in Tokyo prohibit pets, cat cafés became the preferred method for people to get their kitty fix. In December 2014, after a few successful pop-up cat cafés, New York got its first permanent version: Meow Parlour. Patrons can come cuddle with felines, have a pastry and even adopt a cat! Reservations are recommended.

59

Nagley's General Store

"He's the mayor; it's not a joke. I know it's ridiculous, but the town is run really well."
—ASHLEY KEARNS, LOCAL PIZZA SHOP EMPLOYEE TO CNN

LOCATED IN Talkeetna, Alaska, Nagley's General Store has the honor of being home to the town's mayor: a tailless cat named Stubbs. According to rumors, Mayor Stubbs won the office at just three months old as a write-in candidate in 1997 and has remained the mayor ever since—NPR has since debunked this rumor, pointing out that as a historical district Talkeetna does not technically have a mayor, and so there was no election. Regardless, the people of this small Alaskan town have considered Stubbs to be their mayor, at least in spirit, for the last two decades.

Mayor Stubbs enjoying a nap, pictured right.

Radiator

THOUGH FIREPLACES have undeniable charm (especially with a cat curled up in front of one), they were not ideal for heating homes: Most of the heat went up the chimney, and chimney fires posed a serious risk, especially in homes built close together or with thatched roofs. In the 1850s, a Prussian-born Russian man named Franz San Galli invented a solution: the radiator. A radiator is much safer than an open fire and also much more efficient at heating a home, unless a cat happens to be hogging all the warmth by lounging on top of it.

61

The New York E Train

IN JULY 2015, a cat named George broke free from his leash on the platform of the Canal Street station and jumped down onto the tracks. His owner was able to stop an incoming E train from proceeding, and within half an hour, an NYPD officer rescued George. According to Officer Brian Kenny: "I picked him up; he reached for both of my shoulders like a baby. He almost hugged me." George reportedly delayed more than 80 trains and is not the only cat to have wreaked havoc in the New York subway system: Cats have been rescued from the tracks in at least three different boroughs.

Cat Memorial Stone

"Until one has loved an animal a part of one's soul remains unawakened."
—ANATOLE FRANCE

WHILE NOT as grand as the cat memorials of Ancient Egypt
or even the bronze statues some famous cats have received,
many modern cat owners choose to mark their cat's passing
and place of rest with a commemorative stone—a reflection of
how even though we no longer consider cats to be deities, many
people still develop deep attachments to their feline friends.
This practice has become more popular in the age of Etsy, with
countless shop owners promising personalized, hand-etched
stones by which to remember Fluffy, Tybalt and Mr. Buttertoots.

LICKI Brush

"Lick your cat. Like a cat."
—LICKI Brush Slogan

IN 2016, cats and their owners gained the ability to bond with one another on a whole new level. The LICKI brush is a silicone tongue, meant to let cat owners bite down on one end and "lick" their pets with the other, without the potential downside of later choking on a hairball. The manufacturers argue licking your cat is a good bonding experience, citing the "immediate benefits of mutual grooming." Cat owners seem to agree—the Kickstarter for this project raised more than $50,000, and multiple YouTube videos of people licking their kitties have gone viral.

64

Crazy Cat Lady Action Figure

FOR MORE than 30 years, a company called Archie McPhee/ Accoutrements has been manufacturing decidedly odd products, including the Cat Bonnet, the Inflatable Unicorn Horn for Cats and the Crazy Cat Lady Action Figure. Including six felines (eight if you count the one slung around her shoulders and one in her pocket) and a pink-robed woman with a "wild look" in her eyes, this product pokes fun at "crazy cat ladies," a common media trope and pejorative term for any single woman who owns multiple cats. However, a 2017 study published in the journal *Psychological Medicine* has shown that there is no link between cat ownership in childhood and psychotic symptoms— so the joke's on all those catless critics!

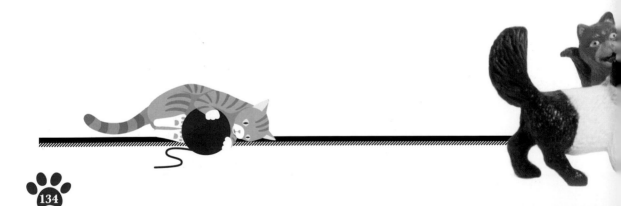

Archie McPhee

CRAZY CAT LADY
ACTION FIGURE

COMES WITH 6 CATS!

WARNING:
...ZARD – Small Parts.
...nder 3 years.

135

Claws Encounters

Though cat caretakers strive to provide their charges with an array of toys and furniture to keep them occupied, nothing seems to match the allure of claiming—and often shredding— what they're not supposed to have.

65

Toilet Paper

THOUGH TOILET paper was first commercially produced in 1857, it took a little more than 20 years for companies to begin selling it in rolls. In 1890, the Scott Paper Company introduced SCOTT® Brand Tissue at the bargain price of 10 cents for a roll of 1,000 sheets. Originally deemed a medical product, print ads were used to explain the new commodity and quell embarrassment over buying such a personal item. Incidentally, cats have never seemed to be embarrassed by their shredding, unfurling or strewing of toilet paper, even when it becomes scattered about the house.

66

Cardboard Paper Towel Tube

SHORTLY AFTER inventing the toilet paper roll, Arthur Scott of Scott Paper Company heard about a school teacher distributing soft paper to sick students to prevent them from using cloths multiple times and spreading their germs to other students. Scott realized the potential in his leftover scraps from toilet paper production and invented the "Sani-Towel," sheets of disposable towels that became prevalent in public restrooms. In 1931, Scott Paper Company realized the potential for these towels in the kitchen and repackaged them in large perforated rolls, similar to their toilet paper. Naturally, the bigger the roll, the bigger the tube within it, and soon cats everywhere had a new and thrilling item to nibble, chase and bat around.

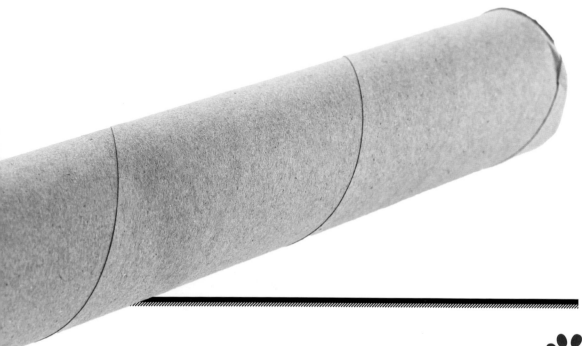

Shopping Bag

THOUGH HUMANS have fashioned bags out of animal hide and cloth for thousands of years, the disposable paper shopping bag was not invented until 1852, by a man named Francis Wolle in Jacobsburg, Pennsylvania. Due to their cleanliness and convenience, paper bags remained the standard way to carry groceries and other goods for more than 100 years, until the invention of the plastic bag in 1977. Though this cost-effective change would hold a lot of implications for the environment, it was likely all the same to cats, who generally enjoy hiding themselves within any errant bags left lying on the floor.

Glass of Water

INITIALLY OPAQUE, glass was first made 5,000 years ago in Western Asia, Egypt, Mycenae and Crete. Starting around the 16th century B.C., glass was used to make vessels, though it would not become transparent for another 800 years after that. Transparent glass became a very popular choice for drinkware and a near-synonym for the word "cup," likely because of its ability to hold liquids of various temperatures and our desire to see the contents within. However, there is one drawback: Glass is extremely prone to breaking, especially when pushed off a ledge by a curious cat. According to Dr. H. Ellen Whiteley, a veterinarian and author of four books on pet behavior, cats prod things to see if they're potential prey.

Of course, most housecats learn rather quickly that water glasses are not prey, but they still enjoy knocking them over out of boredom or in order to get their owner's attention.

69

Fish Bowl

BOTH HUMANS and cats have always found staring at fish to be a bit hypnotic—Ancient Roman, Egyptian and Chinese civilizations all created artificial ponds, and not just as a way to store fresh dinner. Ornamental fish remained popular for centuries, but the practice of keeping them indoors was not refined until the invention of the glass aquarium in 1832. This innovation acknowledged the balance required between fish, plants and oxygen—most fish won't survive very long in just any bowl filled with water, especially in a home with a cat. That being said, a properly protected fish bowl can captivate a bored house cat for hours on end.

Cardboard Box

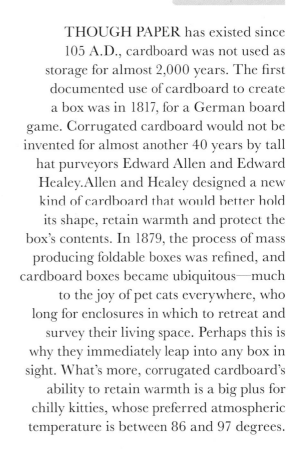

THOUGH PAPER has existed since 105 A.D., cardboard was not used as storage for almost 2,000 years. The first documented use of cardboard to create a box was in 1817, for a German board game. Corrugated cardboard would not be invented for almost another 40 years by tall hat purveyors Edward Allen and Edward Healey.Allen and Healey designed a new kind of cardboard that would better hold its shape, retain warmth and protect the box's contents. In 1879, the process of mass producing foldable boxes was refined, and cardboard boxes became ubiquitous—much to the joy of pet cats everywhere, who long for enclosures in which to retreat and survey their living space. Perhaps this is why they immediately leap into any box in sight. What's more, corrugated cardboard's ability to retain warmth is a big plus for chilly kitties, whose preferred atmospheric temperature is between 86 and 97 degrees.

71

Jewelry

JUST AS cats seem to have always been fixated on toying with their caretakers, humans have long been fascinated with the idea of decorating themselves. Even before precious metals were discovered, humans fashioned jewelry from shells, fishbones and colored pebbles. By the third millennium B.C., Sumerians had begun crafting lavish diadems, earrings, necklaces, rings and bracelets from gold, silver, lapis lazuli and other precious metals. While people treasure their jewelry for various aesthetic reasons, cats seem to pass judgment purely based on how much a piece dangles, and how much it would annoy their owner if they were to begin chewing on it.

Shoelaces

THOUGH ANTHROPOLOGISTS estimate that people have been wearing some form of shoes for 40,000 years, the highly decomposable nature of most early footwear has made evidence of that fact quite rare. The oldest leather shoe in the world, and the earliest example of shoes with laces (as opposed to woven sandals), is dated to approximately 3500 B.C. Modern shoelaces often incorporate synthetic fibers, but throughout history shoelaces have been made from leather, cotton, jute and hemp. Regardless of material, few cats can resist clawing at their owner's shoelaces—particularly while they are being tied and especially if said owners are running late for work.

Socks

THE VERY first socks were likely animal skins, which people would tie around their ankles. By the year 100 A.D. Romans were wearing udones, a rudimentary sock sewn from animal hair. And by the 3rd century A.D., Egyptians had begun knitting socks. Socks (or rather, stockings) were considered a status symbol for hundreds of years, until fashion trends finally relegated the sock to a more humble status: A piece of basic clothing that is rarely seen. Though people generally take their socks for granted and do little more than shrug when one is eaten by the dryer, cats delight in finding a single sock that has been shoved under the bed. Socks are easy to carry and bat around and, even better, a dirty sock smells like its owner—a smell that cats often find comforting.

74

Pants

THE OLDEST known pair of trousers were worn by horse riders in Central Asia, approximately 3,000 years ago. In fact, the question of why people switched from wearing tunics or kilts to pants revolves around the domestication of the horse— men who rode horses wore pants, and men who rode horses won wars, making them the heroes, celebrities and style arbiters of their communities. The trend can be seen time and again throughout history: Japanese civilian men and women traditionally wore kimonos while the samurai who fought in battles wore trousers; Roman soldiers began wearing pants and riding horses after being beaten by Hannibal and his cavalry; the Plains Indians wore kilts until Europeans introduced them to horses. However, while wearing pants is connected with an advantage in battle, anyone who has owned a kitten that likes to climb is also intimately aware of their drawbacks.

Curtains

"The key to a successful new relationship between a cat and human is patience." –Susan Easterly

THOUGH WINDOW curtains did not become common until the English began using them in the late 16th century, draperies were used as partitions in drafty English homes for much longer—they were especially useful in reducing the chill produced from cold stone walls. Window curtains became popular by the end of the 18th century, with various fabrics, swags, tails and tie-backs being introduced to interior design—and to cats, as even more invitations to climb, scratch and shred the window treatments.

Scratched Upholstery

"The cat lives alone, has no need of society, obeys only when she pleases, pretends to sleep that she may see more clearly and scratches everything on which she can lay her paw."

—François-René de Chateaubriand

LONG A symbol of style and comfort, upholstered seats were rare until the 17th century. Upholstered settees, the sofa's fancier ancestor, began appearing in wealthy homes during this time, and the first fully upholstered sofa, except for the legs, was a Chippendale camelback sofa made in the 18th century. Though it's difficult to say when cats first began scratching upholstery, it likely began happening with much greater frequency once people started keeping their clawed kitties indoors at all times—something that would not happen on a wide scale until cat litter became commercially available in the 1950s.

Christmas Tree

BORROWING PAGAN and Roman traditions of using evergreen branches and trees to celebrate winter festivals, Christians likely began celebrating with Christmas trees about 1,000 years ago. Two Latvian cities argue over who had the first documented use of a Christmas tree—Tallinn claims it had the first tree in 1441, while Riga claims their tree from 1510 was actually the first. But it was Martin Luther who may have been the first to bring a tree indoors, in the early 1500s. Soon after, people began decorating trees with ornaments, which is when they probably became irresistible to cats. Those that managed to suppress their instinctive need to climb were then presented with another challenge: Ignoring extremely shiny, chaseable and breakable objects hanging from every branch.

USB Cord

USB, OR UNIVERSAL SERIAL BUS, is a kind of connection invented in the mid 1990s. It gradually replaced previous connectors such as serial and parallel ports, making the USB the standard for connecting flash drives, printers, phones and various other accessories to computers and chargers. As a relatively inexpensive innovation, the

USB cord is also easily replaced if a teething kitten chews it to bits—though some cats never grow out of this habit. Pet owners who want to avoid that outcome for their USB cords (and stop their cat from potentially electrifying itself) often try to hide the cords, make them distasteful with hot sauce or soap or even purchase protective cord covers.

79

Roomba

THE FIRST upright, portable, motor-powered vacuum cleaner was invented in 1907 by James Murray Spangler, a janitor living in Ohio. Almost 100 years later, the vacuum world was revolutionized onced again: Introduced in 2002 by iRobot, the Roomba is the most iconic—but not the first—autonomous robotic vacuum cleaner (the prohibitively expensive Electrolux Trilobite, since discontinued, was introduced the year prior). Perhaps Roomba owes some of its continued success to cats, who generally seem to assume the apparatus exists as a meandering form of kitty transportation. Soon after YouTube was launched in 2005, cat owners began posting videos of their cats and kittens riding on the vacuums, giving people who dislike cleaning up cat hair yet another reason to purchase a Roomba.

Laptop

MANY HISTORIANS say the Osborne 1, invented in 1981, was the first truly portable computer. However, because most people likely did not want to spend almost $2,000 to carry around a computer that weighed nearly 24 pounds and only had a 5-inch screen, its success was short-lived. Still, the '80s featured a huge growth spurt for personal computer technology—companies such as Compaq, Apple, Zenith and Microsoft each released their own versions of laptops, and by the mid-1990s, laptops were starting to become more affordable and accessible to business people, students and sleepy cats alike.

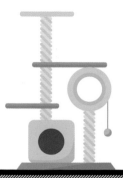

Cat Culture

Whether it's because of their big eyes, soft bellies or aloof attitudes, cats have infiltrated—and arguably dominated—almost every aspect of pop culture.

Monopoly Cat Token

FIRST SOLD by Parker Brothers in 1935, and based on a game called The Landlord's Game patented in 1904, Monopoly is a classic American board game. Though special edition tokens have been released before in Monopoly's history, and tokens have been traded out—a lantern, purse and rocking horse were retired by the 1950s, replaced by the Scottie dog, a figure riding a horse and a wheelbarrow— 2013 marked the first time the public was able to weigh in on the decision. Monopoly left the choice of the iron's successor up to the internet, which was given the options of a robot, helicopter, diamond ring, guitar and a cat. Unsurprisingly for a web-based election, the cat emerged the victor.

Cats, Lions, and a Dragon

"This animal species, of which the lion is the prince because of its spinal column which is flexible...."
—LEONARDO DA VINCI,
INCOMPLETE NOTES ALONG BOTTOM OF DRAWING

DRAWN IN pen and ink c. 1513–18, Leonardo da Vinci's drawings of more than 20 cats and lions, and a single dragon, seem to be an attempt to capture the incredible flexibility of cats—and the imagined flexibility of dragons. While there certainly weren't any dragons roaming around for da Vinci to sketch, he may have used live models for the lions, which were easily found in Florence during this time. As symbols of the city, lions were kept in a cage behind the Palazzo della Signoria (now known as the Palazzo Vecchio).

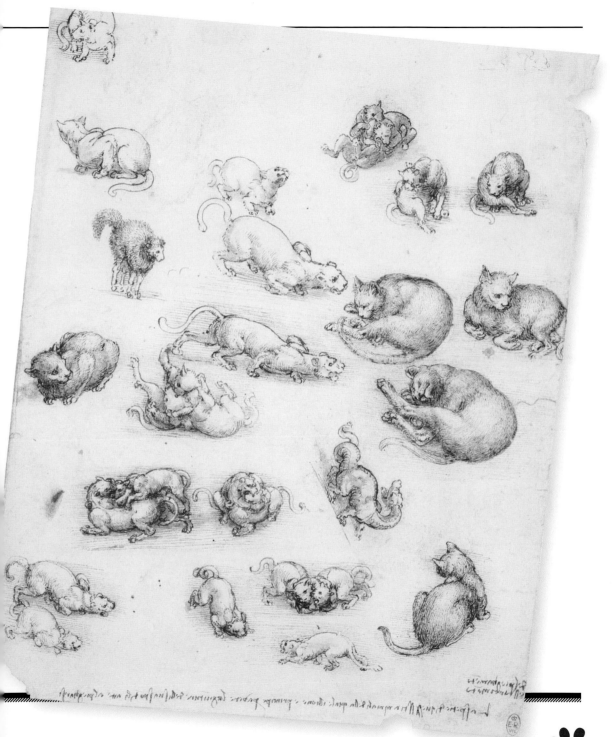

83

Le Maître Chat, ou le Chat Botté (Puss in Boots) Storybook

MOST OF today's children are familiar with DreamWorks's Puss in Boots, a character introduced in 2004. But this fairy tale is at least 450 years old: The oldest written version of Puss in Boots dates back to the 1550s, by Italian author Giovanni Francesco Straparola. However, it was French author Charles Perrault's 1697 version that stood the test of time. His collection of fairy tales was called "Histoires ou contes du temps passé" with the subtitle "Les Contes de ma mère l'Oye," or in English, "Stories of Past Times: Mother Goose Tales." The DreamWorks version goes on quite a few adventures that Perrault never wrote about, but his flair for deceit and fashionable footwear remain unchanged.

LE CHAT BOTTÉ

84

The Cheshire Cat

"'I don't like the looks of it,' said the King, 'however, it may kiss my hand, if it likes.' 'I'd rather not,' the Cat remarked."
  –LEWIS CARROLL, *ALICE'S ADVENTURES IN WONDERLAND*

PERHAPS THE most iconic feline in modern literature, the Cheshire Cat perfectly encapsulates many of the more frustrating qualities possessed by cats: He's mysterious, elusive, sassy and also a bit mad. Published in 1865, Lewis Carroll's classic children's book *Alice's Adventures in Wonderland* has inspired dozens of adaptations in television, film, live theatre and even comic books—thanks, in no small part, to a cat with an especially wide grin and the ability to stand on its head.

85

Le Chat Noir Poster

A LONG-WHISKERED black cat with piercing eyes has helped the poster advertising Le Chat Noir eclipse the fame of the establishment itself, becoming an iconic symbol of Paris. Le Chat Noir opened on November 18, 1881, in the Montmartre district and is thought to be the first modern cabaret. The show was extremely popular for more than 15 years, with the last performance taking place in January of 1897.

Felix the Cat Poster

CREATED BY Otto Messmer and Pat Sullivan in 1919, Felix the Cat is one of the most famous entertainers from the silent film era, alongside the likes of Charlie Chaplin and Buster Keaton. Known for his jaunty walk and impish antics, Felix has been immortalized in short films, comics, a television show, countless toys, a 1988 feature film and as the mascot of a Los Angeles Chevrolet dealership.

Detective Comics Featuring Batman and Robin #211

"So Batman trailed me! Well, he'll learn that those who bother cats can get scratched!"
—CATWOMAN

THE ORIGINAL Catwoman/Selina Kyle was introduced in 1940 in *Batman #1*, and has generally been portrayed as an anti-heroine with whom Batman shares a perpetual love-hate relationship, as most people do with cats. Skilled in martial arts and an effortless cat burglar, Catwoman's abilities are decidedly feline: She's clever, flexible and agile, with a perfect sense of balance and speed. Her character walks a fine line between good and evil; never depicted as a killer, Catwoman has managed to rank on both IGN's lists of "Top 100 Villains" and "Top 100 Comic Book Heroes." In "The Jungle Cat-Queen," released in 1954 and one of Catwoman's classic stories, she's more foe than friend to Batman: Catwoman steals some valuable jewels, and despite the heros' best efforts to capture her, she manages to get away in the end. Alongside various iterations of her character in comics, Catwoman has been notably portrayed on screens big and small by Eartha Kitt, Michelle Pfeiffer, Anne Hathaway and (in a widely panned production) Halle Berry.

Tom and Jerry

SINCE 1940, people have gotten a good dose of schadenfreude from watching Tom, a typical house cat, attempt to catch Jerry, an atypically clever mouse, often with disastrous results. The endless variations on the simple theme of "cat chases mouse" have been popular for generations; in 1965, edited versions of *Tom and Jerry* shorts began airing on television, and the duo have been a cartoon staple ever since—Warner Bros. even rebooted the cartoon as *Tom and Jerry Tales* in 2006.

Chia Grass Planter, featuring Sylvester and Tweety

KNOWN FOR his trademark lisp, Sylvester James Pussycat Sr., also known as Puddy Cat or just Sylvester, is a heavily awarded *Looney Tunes* character. Three cartoons starring Sylvester have won Oscars; he jointly placed 33rd (with Tweety Bird) in *TV Guide*'s list of 50 greatest cartoon characters of all time, and in 1952, a United States Air Force unit even made Sylvester its personal emblem. On top of this, Sylvester has been used to market various cat products, including 9 Lives cat food and Chia cat grass. Sufferin' succotash, indeed!

Laundry Basket

WHILE BASKET-WEAVING is one of the oldest crafts in human history, it's difficult to say when it began—most baskets were made of materials that easily decompose. However, the practice has been ongoing since at least 27,000 years ago, according to archeological evidence of basketmaking found in the southeastern Czech Republic. Because baskets are so versatile, the idea of a dedicated laundry basket did not become popular until the end of the 19th century. But once the concept took off, the next 50 years were full of innovations: They were made more attractive, more easily hidden or out of stackable plastic. For cats, however, the best innovation is always the addition of fresh, warm laundry—perfect for covering with hair.

THE **CAT**

IN

THE

HAT

FOR
BEGINNING
READERS

By Dr. Seu

91

The Cat in the Hat

IN 1957, the director of the educational division at Houghton Mifflin asked his friend Theodor Seuss Geisel, better known as Dr. Seuss, to take a list of 220 vocabulary words and create a story for children learning to read. The result was *The Cat in the Hat*, which sold more than one million copies in its first three years. Today, the mischievous cat continues to educate children via PBS's show *The Cat in the Hat Knows a Lot About That!*

BASED ON THE NOVEL BY
TRUMAN CAPOTE
MUSIC–HENRY MANCINI

JNT RELEASE

92

Breakfast at Tiffany's

"I'm like Cat here, a no-name slob. We belong to nobody, and nobody belongs to us."

—HOLLY GOLIGHTLY

THOUGH HIS credits have various names, the cat actor best known as Orangey is the only feline to have been honored with two PATSY (Picture Animal Top Star of the Year) Awards the animal version of the Oscars—for his work as Cat in *Breakfast at Tiffany's* (1961) and the titlular role in *Rhubarb* (1951). Organized by the American Humane Association, PATSY Awards were discontinued in 1986 due to lack of funds. But since 2011, the organization has continued to award animal actors who excel in their craft with Pawscars. In 2016, feline actors John and Orion won the award for "Best Repurring Cat Performance" for their joint performance as Buttercup in *The Hunger Games* franchise.

93

You Only Live Twice

IN THE 1967 Bond film *You Only Live Twice*, Sean Connery's James Bond faces off against Ernst Stavro Blofeld, a supervillain who is always seen stroking a white cat (which, incidentally, may have up to nine lives). This image stuck with audiences so much that, just as a witch is rarely seen without her familiar, stroking a cat has become a trope of villainous characters. Right-hand cats have made their way into classic films and television shows such as *The Smurfs*, *Enter the Dragon* and, of course, the spy-spoof *Austin Powers: International Man of Mystery*.

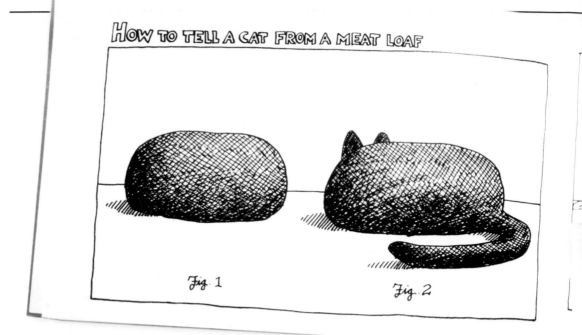

HOW TO TELL A CAT FROM A MEAT LOAF

Fig. 1   Fig. 2

Cat, by B. Kliban

"One hell of a nice animal, frequently mistaken for a meat loaf."

— DEFINITION OF A CAT, B. KLIBAN.

IN 1975, B. Kliban published a book of cartoons about cats that resonated deeply with just about anyone who's ever shared a home with one. Kliban's distinctively odd, humorous and not conventionally cute style of illustrating cats quickly proved popular and was plastered all over calendars, greeting cards, umbrellas, T-shirts and more, creating a $50 million industry during the mid-1980s.

cat (kat), n. [pl. CATS (kats) AS. catte, akin to G. katze < LL. cattus, etc., all via Celt.; prob. IE. base *qat-, to bear young, seen in L. catulus. 1. a small, lithe, soft-furred animal, domesticated since ancient times, and often kept as a pet or for killing mice. 2. . . .
BKliban

The First *Garfield* Comic Strip

ON JUNE 19, 1978, readers of 41 different newspapers across the U.S. were introduced to Garfield, the heavyset pet cat of a cartoonist. Creator Jim Davis originally intended to call his comic *Jon*, but initial reactions persuaded him to shift the focus to the sarcastic cat instead. Today, *Garfield* is a Guinness World Record holder—not for most lasagna eaten by a feline, but because the comic is the most syndicated in the world, appearing in more than 2,500 newspapers and journals.

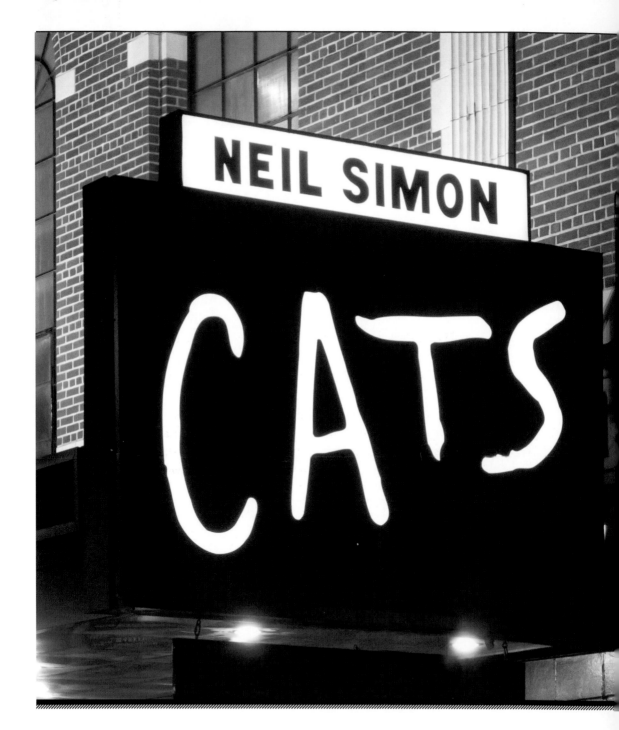

Cats Marquee

BASED ON T.S. Eliot's 1939 collection of poems, *Old Possum's Book of Practical Cats*, and featuring some of Andrew Lloyd Webber's most beloved songs, *Cats* was first staged in London in 1981 and then debuted on Broadway in 1982. The show won seven Tony awards in 1983, including Best Musical—not bad for a production that puts more emphasis on spandex and catlike movements than its plot. The fourth-longest running show on the Great White Way (the casts of *Cats* put on an incredible 7,485 performances over the course of 18 years), it closed in 2000 but was revived in 2016, to mixed reviews. Much like the felines this play is inspired by, *Cats* often inspires deep feelings of either love or hatred in theater-goers.

Kattenkabinet Collection

IN 1990, a man named Bob Meijer founded a museum in commemoration of his pet, a ginger cat named after American banker John Pierpont Morgan. Located in Amsterdam, Kattenkabinet—or Cat Cabinet, in English—is filled with artists' depictions of cats, making it the perfect rendezvous for any cat lover visiting the area. Among the various paintings, drawings, sculptures and posters procured by Meijer is a portrait of J.P. Morgan himself (the cat, not the banker) and framed dollar bills specially printed with the feline's portrait.

201

MUTTS Comic Strip

SINCE 1994, cartoonist Patrick McDonnell's creations have been challenging the assumption that cats and dogs can't be friends. Starring Earl the mutt and Mooch the cat, *MUTTS* is a heartwarming comic that explores the humor in everyday situations and the relationship between cats, dogs and their guardians. The popular comic strip is printed in more than 700 newspapers in 20 countries—not bad for a cat with a lisp.

204

I made you a cookie...

but I eated it.

best sock evar

I Can Has Cheezburger?

ARGUABLY THE meme that opened the floodgates to all other cat memes, not to mention the (thankfully) short-lived trend of internet cat-speak, was a 2007 image of a slightly crazed-looking British Shorthair known as "Happy Cat" with "I can has cheezburger?" plastered in white bold text above him. The father of all "LOLcats," Happy Cat paved the way for Grumpy Cat, Ceiling Cat, Hover Cat, Lime Cat, Business Cat, Monorail Cat and many, many more. LOLcats memes took off so quickly that an entire book of them was published in 2008, with considerable success of its own—it sold more than 160,000 copies.

MAKING ROUNDS
WITH
OSCAR

"I love this book."
—Sara Gruen,
author of
Water for Elephants

*The Extraordinary Gift
of an Ordinary Cat*

DAVID DOSA, M.D.

100

Making Rounds With Oscar

ON TOP of incredible night vision and an exact sense of the moment breakfast is late, cats may have one more mysterious ability: sensing when a person is about to die. Published by Dr. David Dosa in 2009, *Making Rounds With Oscar* tells the story of a cat who has an uncanny sense for predicting which nursing home residents are about to pass. Adopted as a kitten by the Steere House Nursing & Rehabilitation Center in Providence, Rhode Island, Oscar began visiting patients on the third floor shortly before his first birthday. Though it took the staff a while to notice it—residents passing in a nursing home is hardly unexpected—Oscar's selective visits were strongly correlated with a resident's final hours. Once the staff recognized this pattern, they could rely on this incredible kitty as an early warning system, giving them extra time to notify family members and increase hospice services. While nobody can explain the unusual behavior with any certainty (perhaps he carries a kitty curse), Dr. Dosa has speculated that Oscar may be reacting to chemical changes or the patient's lack of movement.

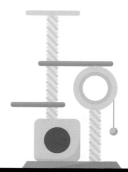

The Creation of cAt-dam

Here We, Zarathustra the Cat, reveal to the world the original version of the famous Michelangelo fresco that *should* (if there were any justice in the world) be on view in the Sistine Chapel today: *The Creation of cAt-dam*.

A bit of background: In the Hebrew language "ādām" means "human" and is linked to its triliteral root אדם (A-D-M), meaning "red," "fair," "handsome." OMG, why can't you humans see it! It's so evident! Adam was a ginger Cat!

Michelangelo, *The Creation of cAt-dam*

59

Fat Cat Art

"...I thought, 'What can I do with Zarathustra, because my mother spoilt him and he's so fat.'"   —SVETLANA PETROVA, *FAT CAT* ARTIST, TO THE BBC

FOLLOWING HER mother's death in 2008, Russian artist Svetlana Petrova found herself adopting her mother's cat, Zarathustra, and had the idea to superimpose the 22-pound orange tabby into famous works of art. Zarathustra—shown falling out of Mona Lisa's arms, cuddled alongside Venus of Urbino, pawing at a cheeseburger placed on the iconic pitchfork in American Gothic—quickly became an internet sensation. In 2015, Petrova published a 250-page book filled with images of the fat, furry cat taking over classic works of art. And the world is better for it.

Fat Cat Art

Famous Masterpieces Improved by a Ginger Cat with Attitude

Svetlana Petrova and
Zarathustra the Cat

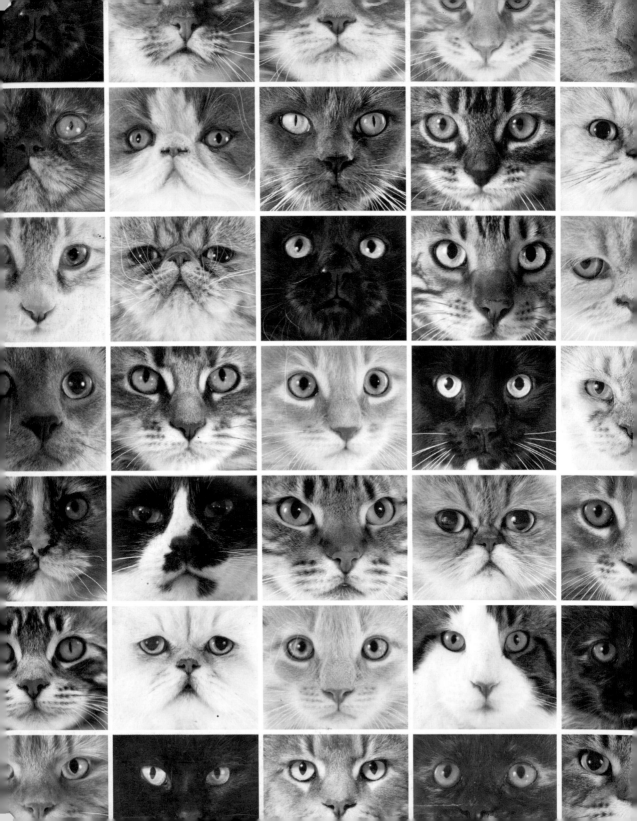